"An invaluable resource of stories and theological insights from two leaders who obviously know something about staying in the city and about learning to see and tell what God is doing there."

— EMMANUEL KATONGOLE
Kroc Institute,
University of Notre Dame

"Cities are now hip and cool, drawing a new and sometimes controversial wave of urbanites. *Stay in the City* tells the stories of those who are not new converts to urban life but have stayed and have learned that staying is part of their own thriving as they contribute to the flourishing of the city. I will recommend this volume widely."

— JUDE TIERSMA WATSON
Fuller Theological Seminary

Stay in the City

*How Christian Faith
Is Flourishing
in an Urban World*

Mark R. Gornik *&* Maria Liu Wong

WILLIAM B. EERDMANS PUBLISHING COMPANY
GRAND RAPIDS, MICHIGAN

Wm. B. Eerdmans Publishing Co.
2140 Oak Industrial Drive NE, Grand Rapids, Michigan 49505
www.eerdmans.com

26 25 24 23 22 21 20 19 18 17   1 2 3 4 5 6 7 8 9 10

ISBN 978-0-8028-7404-7

Library of Congress Cataloging-in-Publication Data

Names: Gornik, Mark R., author. | Wong, Maria Liu, 1976- author.
Title: Stay in the city : how Christian faith is flourishing in an urban
    world / Mark R. Gornik & Maria Liu Wong.
Description: Grand Rapids, Michigan : William B. Eerdmans Publishing
    Company, [2017] | Includes bibliographical references.
Identifiers: LCCN 2017029707 | ISBN 9780802874047 (pbk. : alk. paper)
Subjects: LCSH: City churches—New York—New York. | City missions—
    New York—New York. | New York (N.Y.)—Church history—20th century. |
    New York (N.Y.)—Church history—21st century.
Classification: LCC BV637 .G627 2017 | DDC 277.47/1083—dc23
    LC record available at https://lccn.loc.gov/2017029707

To Sue, who has stayed in the city

Contents

Foreword

As I read Mark Gornik and Maria Liu Wong's book on the urban church, the word "tapestry" kept coming to mind. A tapestry is often called "rich" because of how variegated, multicolored, elaborate, thick with innumerable designs and depictions, and beautiful it is. You have to stand and gaze at the greatest tapestries for a long time before you begin to see even a fraction of all that is going on. You also usually have to stand in several spots and look at it from different perspectives to even begin to take its measure.

The church in the city is exactly the same, and it is just as hard to take in with one glance. If you are a Christian in the city you are, as it were, only one small part of that tapestry. Or to put it another way, you are looking at it from just one vantage point. It is almost impossible to see all that God is doing through his church in the city around you. There are not just the ordinary divisions between mainline Protestant, Catholic, and Orthodox, evangelical and Pentecostal. There are also churches with different racial and national backgrounds, plus those led by first- or second-generation immigrant leaders, and the intentionally multiethnic congregations. There are churches among professionals, blue-collar workers, and the poor, and many that, gladly, seek to incorporate all the classes. It has been rightly quipped that if you don't like big cities you will not like the New Jerusalem. Here indeed are those from every tongue, tribe, people, and nation praising God (Rev. 7:9). The future heavenly city is best glimpsed in our earthly cities today.

That's Mark and Maria's purpose in this short volume—to give you a look at the present and future city of God in all its wondrous variety. As I said, it is almost impossible to really see it all. I've lived in New York City for going on three decades, and I am often impressed with (still) how little of God's church here I've been able to know. But Mark and Maria have done something remarkable here. They give dozens of little snapshots of the urban church, but across an extraordinarily wide range of neighborhoods, traditions, and nationalities. I don't know of anyone who could give us as complete a picture as they have.

Christians who already live in cities should read this book just to revel in that of which they are already a part. Christians who are considering living in cities, or staying in cities longer term, need to read this to be challenged and I hope attracted to the life-long adventure of living and ministering in the city. And even though this is not a how-to manual (it will be followed up with another volume), still you will find named here all the basic practices of urban Christian practice—vocation and service, family life, church community life, ministry in word and deed, sharing of "third" spaces.

Even though its companion volume, *Sense the City*, promises to be more practical and concrete, this book ends with time-tested, high-level principles for long-term fruitfulness. It points out how seamlessly family life, ministry, and our work-for-pay go together.

Urban Christians, more is going on than you know. Praise the God who loves infinite variety, and stay in the city.

TIMOTHY KELLER

Prologue: Urban Christians

On a stretch of blocks known as Shelter Row on Atlantic Avenue in east New York, Brooklyn, one of the city's toughest areas, there is a building on the corner that holds more than individuals in transition. True Holy Church, called the City of Refuge in the community, is a haven where Pastor Vivian, his wife Beverly, and their four children have made a home for those without a home. When the attacks on September 11, 2001, took place, Vivian lost his job on Wall Street. Instead of searching for another job in accounting and finance, he looked at his church's unfinished building, picked up a hammer, and went to work completing it, day after day on the construction site, often on his own.

In a few years, when the pastor of True Holy retired, Vivian was called to be the new pastor, and the church continues to flourish as a good neighbor in the community under his care. Primarily a West Indian immigrant and African American congregation, with ties to Jamaica and London, True Holy Church serves the neighborhood in Brooklyn through mentoring programs, a food pantry, and support for local organizations. And by building up above their sanctuary, they are adding much needed affordable housing to their neighborhood. But most of all, City of Refuge is a place where Christians are living their faith within and beyond the walls of the church building.

Across the city on the Upper West Side of Manhattan, Kari Jo and her husband Cory have made their home a place of welcome and ministry. Having moved to New York City from Kansas City so Cory could attend graduate school in applied physics, they purchased a townhouse with friends, gutting and renovating it floor by floor. They raised their four kids—two boys and two girls—alongside others, with whom they shared their home and lives.

When she was not biking around the city running errands for her family or others, Kari Jo found herself walking alongside other moms and families, many new to the city and adjusting to raising kids in an urban environment. School, work, parenting, and marriage were all daily topics of conversation with these families. Her home, located across the street from the public school where all of her children attended, became Grand Central: at any given moment, hungry teens came through the door looking for brownies and popcorn, or neighbors' children were dropped off for a few hours. This way of life in her home and in Manhattan brought Kari Jo to the staff of Redeemer

Presbyterian Church Downtown, where she directs their ministry to families.

Peter, Miriam, and their daughters live farther north, in East Harlem. Peter grew up in both the Lower East Side and the Bronx. After working for some time as a jeweler, he changed direction, becoming a hospital social worker and also an assistant pastor at the Damascus Christian Church of Hunts Point, part of a Latino Pentecostal movement that includes some two hundred churches throughout North, Central, and South America, and the Caribbean. On Sunday he preaches, and on Monday evenings he is the principal and teacher in the council's Bible Institute. He also serves on the board of a local community development organization in Harlem.

Miriam, who grew up in Harlem and the Bronx and worked in community healthcare for over two decades, leads as a minister at the same church. She also serves as the treasurer (and in the past, as children's ministry leader) at the church and council levels and has brought her administrative and ministry expertise into the arena of urban theological education. Intergenerational worship is an important focus of her congregation. And she leads the congregation through praise dance in worship.

Not far to the west in Harlem, Sister Marylin, a woman religious with the Sisters of St. Ursula who has been living there for over twenty-five years, serves her community as a spiritual director and leads retreats in upstate New York.

As part of her calling, Sister Marylin has also served her neighborhood as a social worker and has worked in the Congo for her religious community. She welcomes others into a larger vision of faith and ministry in the city through a foundational understanding of Ignatian spirituality.

Melissa and Andy, a newly married couple living on the edges of Manhattan's Chinatown community, grew up respectively in Brooklyn and Queens. They met at Chinese Evangel Mission Church, one of many immigrant Chinese churches in the area. While Melissa, a business consultant, grew up in the church, Andy, a mechanic with the New York City Sanitation Department, is the only Christian believer in his predominantly Buddhist family. Andy and Melissa's work with children and youth in the church, and their openness to listening to their elders, fosters an environment that looks to the future of the church at large—creating space for intergenerational conversations and corporate worship.

Rex, born in Harlem but now living in the Bronx, attends the growing Presbyterian Church of Ghana in Harlem, the church of his parents who came to New York from Accra. Even as a young person Rex had potential that was recognized and affirmed by the elders at his church, and now he has been called upon to take on leadership with the worship team and youth ministry there. He also works as an administrator in higher education and is keen on completing further theological education in order to pursue his calling as a pastor to serve young people and families.

While Vivian and Beverly, Kari Jo and Cory, Peter and Miriam, Sister Marylin, Melissa and Andy, and Rex live and work in different parts of the city, attend churches from a range of cultures and traditions, and come from very diverse social backgrounds, they share in common something more profound than any potential differences. Through their experience of Christ, they each heard the Spirit's call to stay in the city. With their families and communities, they are serving fellow New Yorkers and their love for God extends as a blessing to their neighbors, places of work, and worlds of influence.

Pentecostal, Catholic, evangelical, and historic Protestant, they are part of the whole city, urban Christians in the twenty-first century.

Introduction: Stay in the City

This book is for those who are living, seeking to live, and hoping to sustain lives of joy and purpose through practices that undergird thriving faith in a 24/7 urban world. Whether in a small city or large global city, in a changing neighborhood where new restaurants and businesses are arriving, in a community where lives are always in precarious balance, or in a place of prime real estate and executive offices, the vocation of urban Christians begins with presence. It is a calling to be present with and open to God in the local context, attending to what is in front of us with all of our senses. Ministry is theology on the ground, asking and answering questions of faith and life, work and home, love and neighbor in a dynamic, constantly changing urban world that we live in every day.

There is a common assumption that ministry, especially in the city, is first of all what we do: an action or strategy we take, a program we lead, a church we start, a particular word we have to share, or a special place of need to which we must go. But as we consider the stories of Vivian and Beverly, Kari Jo and Cory, Peter and Miriam, Sister Marylin, Melissa and Andy, and Rex, we see through their lives, families, and communities that the foundational practice of ministry in the city is not an activity but waiting on the Spirit, being ready to notice what God is already doing, and then finding ways to join in with our unique gifts and callings.

As we discover in the Gospels, staying in the city is about being continually aware of and alert to what God is doing in our midst, to having our assumptions turned upside down and our questions changed, and to the possibility of the unexpected. It is about realizing how little we understand and know about the complexity of our city and life, but even more so, growing from this realization into a deeper, more profound trust in God.

This doesn't mean we are not to be thoughtful, innovative, and creative as the city invites and requires us to be. Instead, it means waiting on God, staying present in the city around us, and discerning ways forward. This is how the Spirit sparks us into the joyful adventure of urban discipleship.

How do we know what to do in ministry? Where do we begin? What do we see God already doing in the city? How do we join in? What do we do when our fears and doubts build in the in-between times as we wait on God?

The Gospel of Luke and its companion volume Acts

invite us to a journey of discerning how we are to proceed.[1] Luke is a carefully developed account of the life and ministry of Jesus. With his inaugural sermon at Nazareth, Jesus lays out his mission and purpose to proclaim the year of the Lord's favor (4:14–21): the healing, saving, and restoring of all things, especially good news for the poor. This is the message of the good news, the coming of the kingdom of God for all of creation, as the background in the prophet Isaiah illuminates. And then a few verses later, Jesus sums up his purpose: "I must proclaim the good news of the kingdom of God to the other cities also; for I was sent for this purpose" (4:43).

The story that Luke then unfolds in the Gospel takes us to the cross, the resurrection, and the ascension of Jesus. But it also closes with an urban great commission, Jesus calling upon his followers not to go to the city, but to stay in the city:

> And see, I am sending upon you what my Father promised; so stay here in the city until you have been clothed with power from on high. (24:49)

The city, with all its noises, activities, transactions, conflicts, passions, uncertainties, cultures, and energies—this is where the risen Jesus tells his disciples to stay and wait for "power from on high," the Spirit. The ascended Christ will still be present through the Spirit, through a people, in the city. As they wait, pray, fast, and anticipate what God will do in the city, the Spirit will come upon a new people called the church, which, in Luke's view, are already dispersed and present among the nations.[2]

This theme appears again and is expanded in the book of Acts, Luke's equally carefully narrated Part Two. Here is where the beginning of the church took place with the sending of the Spirit, and then moved among a people from Jerusalem to Rome, from city to city. It is the ministry of Jesus announced to the city in Luke 4, now carried forth by a new people transformed by Christ as they are dispersed among the nations.[3] However great the challenges the new communities of Christians in the city faced, they carried a message of the kingdom of God (Acts 28:31).[4]

In these times when protests have claimed the streets of cities around the world, Luke 24 is like God holding forth a sign in the city, not as dissent but as an announcement. The words are simple: Stay in the City. Dig In. Love Your City. Keep at It. Wait for the Spirit. And as in the first century, the church today is called to be the "Spirited Art" of God, a people alive in the cities and streets of our world.[5]

*　　　*　　　*

"The twenty-first century is the first urban century in human history," observes the *New York Times* architecture critic Michael Kimmelman, "the first time more people on the planet live in cities than don't."[6] Only two centuries ago, just 3 percent of the world's population lived in cities; today, over 50 percent do so. The urban populations of Africa, Asia, and Latin America keep growing upward and outward, adding new cities, while existing ones spread out into rural landscapes and climb hillsides. Europe is urbanized, and many of North America's cities, once seen as less desirable places to live, are now attractive to growing numbers of people, with immigrants having led the way. Firms with global operations are a strategic factor, and millennials in coastal and now central cities have also played a part.[7] In fact, it may be suprising to learn how much of America is an urban nation, with some 63 percent of Americans living in cities.[8]

Overall, the trend toward global urbanization seems likely to accelerate in decades to come, reaching perhaps more than 70 percent of the world's population. Even as every city is part of a larger global world, however, no two cities are alike, growing in endless shapes and sizes. Some are small, some are mega-metropolises, some are crowded and some underpopulated, and still others are somewhere in between, but each has its unique challenges, opportunities, complexities, and differences.[9] Whether Atlanta or Detroit, Dakar or Dar-es-Salaam, Seoul or Hong Kong, Amsterdam or Toronto, Mexico City or Medellín, every city needs to be understood in terms of its own histories, strengths, and moment in time.[10]

Cities are centers of economic growth, activity, and innovation. They are hubs of education, the arts, and the sciences. Cities are also the forward edge of emergent matters facing our world in the environment and changing climate, culture, housing, and health.[11] And some of the most immense challenges of urban life are faced by the over one billion people who live in favelas, townships, and shantytowns of Africa, Asia, and Latin America. Others live in refugee camps that have become cities. It is no wonder that the United Nations Millennium Development Goals emphasize the sustainability and livability of cities.[12]

Because cities are central to our world, we must also see their vital potential for addressing our future.[13] And even if we don't live in a city, we all have a stake in the future of cities. For we all share a globalized planet where cities draw and connect the world's communications, trade, commerce, food systems, and energy resources.[14] As new themes for urban well-being emerge, such as the green city, smart city, happy city, or welcoming city, our cities will also need to be *learning cities*, with an emphasis on lifelong learning toward sustainability and improved quality of life across all sectors.[15]

* * *

The twenty-first century is also an age of urban Christianity, mirroring the first-century church, which was an urban movement.[16] In this era of intense urban growth and change, most Christians, whether historic Protestant mainline, Catholic, Pentecostal, evangelical, or one of many other varieties, call cities home.[17] Specialized terms like "urban ministry" no longer fit a world where Christian presence and ministry are simply urban by default. We are all part of the ecosystems, cultures, and networks that comprise our urban world.[18]

Whether we are longtime residents or new immigrants, young or old, full-time pastors or church workers that hold other jobs, stay-at-home parents or students, banking executives or building superintendents, health-care workers or artists, the question is no longer if Christians live out their faith in the city, but how.

Stay in the City is about what we see happening in the urban church, and how we understand some of what God is doing in the multiplicity of cities and intersecting life spaces of our urban world. A companion book, *Sense the City*, will offer a more in-depth guide to practices that shape the way we do ministry and find our way in the world. But first, in this book, we need to talk about the fact that cities, once disparaged by so many in the church because of their unique challenges, are where Christian faith must flourish—and is indeed flourishing—as they become the homes for more and more of the world's population. This book is intended for churches and parishes, pastors and parish leaders, parents and students, and others who live their faith in the realities of work and in every sphere of life. It is meant to show some of the many ways that God is at work in a world of urban settings.

Both *Stay in the City* and *Sense the City* are part of our work on the Practices of Ministry in the City, an initiative at City Seminary of New York, undertaken with the generous support of the Lilly Endowment. In this work, we have been gathering and sharing stories, data, and practices that support and encourage the church in our urban age.

What we will be sharing in this book emerges out of this work and the plurality of stories and narratives that are part of and shape City Seminary of New York. Launched in 2003 out of listening to the visions and desires of the Christian community in our city, especially churches, pastors, and leaders from Africa, Asia, and Latin America, City Seminary puts an urban lens on the whole of theological learning. Amidst the fast pace of urban life, we seek to slow down and, in one neighborhood at a time, to bring our faith journeys together and learn the practices of ministry in context. This creates a space that can be transformative, leading to seeing the city, church, and ministry afresh.[19]

The underlying practices that sustain and guide the ministries to which we are called are important.[20] Practices are ways that Christians live out our theological beliefs about God, creation, and redemption in the contexts of our communities. They are the habits and patterns of life that Christians across place, tradition, culture, and time have learned to embrace and enact for the blessing, healing, and flourishing of the world.[21] Practices are passed along to us through the families, churches, communities, and institutions that shape us in the city.

Because there is no single or standard way Christians are faithfully serving Christ in the city, the learning process is critical to us.[22] Rather than simply trying to find answers to existing questions, assuming that there are clear questions with equally clear solutions, we reflect on the complex context of contemporary urban life and its adaptive challenges. We engage in double-loop learning, which means taking a step back to consider if we are actually asking the right questions and to reframe our underlying assumptions and values. Sometimes it is necessary to go further, even into triple-loop learning, reflecting on *learning about learning*, or how we learn in the first place.[23]

Looking ahead to the rest of this book, in chapter 1 we introduce the changes in the church and city that are now part of our North American world. Out of this experience of a diverse church where Christ's reign is proclaimed, we explore the practice of Christian faith in relationship to work, the arts and public faith, family and home.[24] In chapter 2, we move from demographic changes to the ways Christians are practicing their faith in the city across areas of the marketplace and vocation. Chapter 3 emphasizes the role of the arts and culture in relationship to public faith. In chapter 4, we describe how we make a home in the city.

Chapter 5 explores the future of Christian faith in the city through the next generation. In chapter 6, we review key components of faithful and fruitful ministry in the city. And to conclude, we come back to Luke's Gospel and the invitation to stay in the city with joy and work for its blessing, its well-being, and its flourishing.

At the end of each chapter, we offer a series of questions to consider that will help you further reflect on what you experience in the city, and what implications this might have on your practice of ministry. We encourage you to work through them, documenting your answers in a journal or sharing with others in a group together.

Cities are part of God's creation, intended for the flourishing of people and all realms of life. The thriving of cities depends upon the involvement of all. We can share in the work of cities by learning about them, finding ways to participate in their life, and assessing what we can do for the peace of God's world in light of our Christian convictions. As we stay in the city, we can learn to love it, care about its future, and join with others in creating and praying for a more flourishing urban world for all.

All of us are invited to walk together on a journey into discovery of God at work in the city and to respond as God's people to where the Spirit leads in homes, at work, on the streets, and in churches.

Let us each pray for the grace and mercy to be awakened to God's call for our lives and communities.

QUESTIONS TO CONSIDER

- Describe a moment, or a series of incidents, in your life when waiting, rather than going, was the "right" thing to do. What happened? How did you feel during this time? What prompted you to stay rather than go? What did you learn in hindsight?

- Consider what institutions have shaped or informed your life decisions. In what context, or with whom, have you made these choices? Why has this been important?

- What do you think God is calling you to do now? Where is God moving your heart to be? Who is speaking into your life to affirm this call?

Chapter 1

More Is Going On

If you want to experience joyous singing, dancing, and praising God, go to Manida Street in the Hunts Point neighborhood of the South Bronx. Here, nestled among the blocks of residences, shops, restaurants, and warehouses, you will find the Damascus Christian Church of Hunts Point.

Led by pastors Jonathan and Soñia Roque, Damascus doesn't just meet on Sunday afternoons for worship but throughout the week for prayer, Bible study, shared meals, and neighborhood ministry. In fact, each day begins with a 6:00 a.m. call-in prayer meeting by phone. Few churches seem more committed to children and families, with their young people involved in leading the service. Throughout the year, members can attend the Damascus Bible Institute, which offers classes in the Bible and Christian doctrine.

Founded over seventy-five years ago in the Bronx by the ministerial couple Leoncia and Francisco Rosado, the church also began a ministry to men and women with addictions. Today the Council of Damascus Christian Churches includes over two hundred affiliated Damascus churches in the United States and Latin America, just as committed to evangelism, healing, prayer, and worship as when they were founded. Jonathan is not only the pastor of the church but also the bishop of the Council of Damascus Churches.

The people who attend are New Yorkers: families, social workers, police officers, students, educators, and health-care workers. There is no full-time paid staff at Damascus of Hunts Point, and their old building has an endless litany of leaks and problems to be solved. The people of Damascus are all stretched by a faith that moves across work, church, and life. But together they pray without ceasing, carry one another's burdens, and continue to live out the church's founding vision to bless the city and invite all people to begin a new life in Christ. They are a family of brothers and sisters in Christ.

*   *   *

Urban life is marked by constant, unpredictable, and dynamic movement in every direction and space. It is full of surprise and the unexpected. You never know what is going to happen, whom you may meet, or what you will find when you walk out the door in the morning.[1]

Here is one of the biggest surprises in the story of the church in New York, North America, and cities across the world: instead of a place where faith struggles and dies, the twenty-first-century city is where the church comes to grow and thrive. Whether Pentecostal or Catholic, mainline or evangelical, new things are percolating as the church has stayed in the city and responded to God, enacting and proclaiming the gospel.

We see this in our city. Every Sunday, across New York's diverse neighborhoods, from the South Bronx to Manhattan to Queens, Staten Island, and Brooklyn, men and women, children and young people, and families and singles leave their homes and apartments to attend church. By subway or bus, driving a car or walking, they go to meet in schools, recreation centers, traditional church buildings, retired nursing homes, reconfigured hotel buildings, warehouse spaces, and rented meeting halls—anywhere there is a room or a corner to sing, pray, hear the Word, and share a meal.

We see this in cities around the world, from Africa and Asia to Latin America and Europe and North America, on university campuses and on side streets in favelas, in rented rooms or hotels where workers gather midday in Asia, and in the high-rise offices of investment firms across the globe.

Surprised by what God is doing in the city? You are not alone. We are continually. So was the apostle Paul.

As Wayne Meeks showed in *The First Urban Christians*, Paul had a vision for birthing, growing, and connecting together new churches in the Roman urban world.[2] City by city, Paul proclaimed Christ and the kingdom of God, "the mystery hidden for ages in God," as we read in Ephesians (3:9). In Acts 18, we find a description of the apostle Paul's ministry in the city of Corinth, a growing and diverse city in his day. But Paul does not feel things are going so well. He is in the city doing difficult missionary work, proclaiming the gospel alongside people like Priscilla, Aquila, Silas, and Timothy. Together they are working to build new communities of followers of Jesus in the city.

Paul is a servant of God, but perhaps he has fears, disappointments, and uncertainty about the impact of his apostolic work. Into this moment, when he feels alone and discouraged in his efforts, God speaks a word not of judgment but of joy and encouragement: *Do not be afraid. Keep up your ministry. I am with you. I have many people in this city* (Acts 18:9–10).

The language of "I am with you" is the language of God's covenant that began with Abraham. But God is also with Paul through people in the city who are doing things he has no idea about. As *The Message* translation puts it, "You have no idea how many people I have . . . in this city."

This word to Paul recalls what God spoke to Elijah in 1 Kings 19. Fearing for his life, Elijah says to God, "I alone am left." And then God tells him there are seven thousand faithful in Israel. *You are not alone. There is more going on than you know about.*

Like Paul, even a prominent church leader might not know about certain things going on in the city. This is not a judgment, but an invitation to open our vision to see things going on that we might not otherwise perceive. It is also a recognition that the church is in God's hands, not Paul's or ours.[3]

The same is true today. While many churches have stayed faithful in the city across the course of years, particularly African American congregations and parishes, arguably the most important factor for the growth of faith today is global migration between cities. As people have moved around the world and to cities, they are bringing their faith and faith communities with them. Migrations today, born from war and displacement in the Middle East and violence in Central America, for example, bring new challenges to Christian conviction and mission. But in almost any American city today, we can see how immigration over the past decades has brought into view a whole world of Christianity. Every day it seems there are new church signs in Spanish. Churches with congregations rooted in Asia have been established and are growing, while evolving in language and cultural emphasis with new waves of immigration. And African churches are sprouting up everywhere. Overall, migration has been a major net gain for Christianity.[4]

As is so often the case in our global economy and world, the churches that appear to be growing most rapidly are doing so through decentralized networks of relationships and movements across cities. This is not unlike the first century, when the expansion of the church was based on networks of leaders, evangelists, pastors, and families that supported, trained, and helped one another.[5] This was, and is, the ecosystem of urban church life.

I (Mark) remember when my vision and world were turned upside down. It was 1998 and I had just moved from Baltimore to do church and community development work in Harlem. On first view, the neighborhood resembled closely my Sandtown neighborhood in Baltimore, a community marked by population loss, abandoned buildings, and struggles in the basics of life. But I soon began to see something else.

All around us in New York were signs of a new global migration—West Africans from Senegal, Ghana, Gambia, and the Ivory Coast were moving to Harlem and opening new restaurants and businesses. While many of our neighbors were Muslim, I began to wonder if some of the new African immigrants might be Christian.

After doing a little bit of homework, I learned about and visited the Emmanuel Worship Center, an Ethiopian Pentecostal church in the Bronx. The pastor mentioned another church led by African Christians in Brooklyn called the Redeemed Christian Church of God. After visiting them on a Sunday for worship, I learned that Redeemed was part of a ministry based in Lagos with thousands of churches around Africa and the world. One of the next churches I visited was right up the street from the seminary—the Presbyterian Church of Ghana, a church with over 175 years of history in Africa, now bursting at the seams in Harlem.[6]

Over the next ten years, I learned that there were over two hundred African churches in the city. Just as remarkable to me, as I spent my Sundays and more in the neighborhoods and churches of the city, I learned that there are well over two thousand churches in New York founded and led by Christians from Africa, Asia, Latin America, and the West Indies. It was right in front of me, but more was going on than I was able to imagine without a larger way of seeing, thinking, and being bodily present to the work of the Spirit in the city. I needed a new framework to understand how the church was growing and ministry was being practiced.

Today, it is estimated that more than one in ten New Yorkers is a Pentecostal Christian.[7] With New York's history of religious tolerance going back to the Dutch, it is fertile ground for new church life based on the evangel, the good news, to thrive. Like the first-century church, and like early Methodism, today's expansion of the church is based on networks of leaders, evangelists, pastors, and families that support, train, and help one another.

In Ephesians, Paul emphasizes the unity of the church.

The body of Christ is the abundance of God's salvation expressed in one new people of peace. As the historian of Christian mission Andrew Walls observes, it is only by listening to and learning from one another in the diversity of all of the cultures, languages, and histories where Christ is being formed that we can reach the fullness of Christ.[8] When this occurs, it is the gift of an Ephesians moment.

But amidst such diversity and change, we may also think of the differences between us. In Philippians 3, Paul recognizes a variety of ways in which God is working through people. He knows that Christians don't all do things the same way, but all are on a journey to seek the kingdom of God. In the midst of such Christian growth and diversity, Paul's challenge is a basic one: to hold fast to what has been attained and do everything in the name of Jesus.

The church has stayed in the city, getting used to surprises and waiting on God to move. This is good news indeed.

QUESTIONS TO CONSIDER

- What words, images, or phrases come to mind when you consider the church in the city? Do you see the city as a place where the church can grow and flourish, or otherwise? Why?

- What experience have you had with Christians from other traditions and cultures? Have you had the opportunity to worship outside of your home church, and if so, what has your experience been?

- Think back to a moment when you were discouraged when your calling or ministry plan did not turn out the way you thought it would. What did you learn about yourself, about God, and about others through that experience? What might you have done differently in retrospect?

Chapter 2

Whatever You Do

Bola, a banker in midtown Manhattan, labors long hours in the banking industry, navigating the complexities of local needs and the global economy. Since moving to New York from Nigeria, she has come to be known not only for her ability to do good work but also for her openness to pray for and with those who are in need. Bola also ministers in her Pentecostal home church, and has initiated an interdenominational women's ministry on Good Fridays. In all these things she seeks to live with integrity, bringing her love for Christ into every area of her work and life.

Janet and Ann are food entrepreneurs in Williamsburg, Brooklyn. Since starting a business bottling their family's award-winning Korean barbeque marinade recipe made with all-natural ingredients, these two sisters have brought together their missional understanding of family and work. They also partner with a local ministry by supporting survivors of human trafficking.

Alan works in public life. He has always been committed to the well-being of the city through service such as helping support young black males, and he currently works to support families in the education system. He makes choices to serve communities in need. Alan strives to live his faith at work, at home, and in his neighborhood.

What are we to do with our lives? Where does our passion lie as we look both at who we are and at our world? How do we make a coherent whole out of the many parts of our lives—family, work, community, and church?

As human beings, we have a built-in need to understand, to make categories, and to bracket information so we can make sense of things. But when we do this, we often separate faith and work, Sunday and the rest of the week, the sacred and the secular.

Vocation is the idea that the Spirit works through life experiences, gifts, identities, opportunities, and needs in the world in order to lead each of us to discover and live a purposeful life for our common well-being.[1] We are not just called to the place with the "greatest need." Rather, after we have listened to God and to the wisdom of others, we find our vocation in the place we believe God wants us to serve, whether it is Wall Street or a grocery store, school or home.

Bola, Alan, Janet, Ann, and many others like them are engaging every day with questions of faith and the marketplace. But as they do so, they are not drawing lines between work and ministry and life. They are seeking to be who God made them to be, and to be faithful to the work and place where God has called them to serve the kingdom.[2] Instead of ministry as something just a "pastor" or church leader does, we are seeing ministry and vocation encompassing the whole of who we are, twenty-four hours a day, seven days a week.

One can be a minister in a church and work in business—both can be places of ministry, neither elevated over the other. There can also be seasons in our lives in which one may be emphasized more than the other, but there is an integration of our days and weeks, a purpose to everything we do as we live out our vocation in different spheres, each one reflecting back on the other.

We see this for urban pastors, especially among newer immigrant churches. Rarely is there remuneration for church work, and pastors often hold one or more paying jobs. But they don't see one as ministry and the other as work. There is a single calling and purpose; both are work and both are ministry. For this reason, the term "bi-vocational ministry," which can elevate ministry over work, may not be the best term to use.

And interestingly, without being used as a strategy, the workplace is a key means of sharing faith. It is not just that people are more open to change in the city or at work. As people share their stories in natural ways, there is an opportunity for conversation and prayer, for listening and sharing life. In this way, faith and work also go together in cities.

*   *   *

Looking back, it is no coincidence that early Christianity grew and expanded in the city. Cities then and now are places where people from different cultures meet and new cultures are formed in every area of life. Saskia Sassen, a leading urban sociologist, speaks of city-ness, the continual meeting of different people, ideas, and events that happens in a city.[3] Cities are messy places, and city life includes the daily effort that goes into where we live, how we work, how we get around, and how we engage with people we meet.[4]

The early church was in the city not just because it was such an effective place for ministry, or because it was where culture could be most impacted. The city was where the church was able to discover the richness of its own identity. Christianity needed the diversity, the density, and the city-ness of the city to flourish, to push it into working through new questions, ideas, and ways of life.

Christians as city dwellers sought to learn what being "in Christ" entailed for their families, lifestyles, eating habits, public actions, and relationships with their religiously diverse neighbors, whether in Corinth or in Rome.[5] In Acts, we find Christian faith as it was first emerging in the Roman Empire. As we read throughout Acts, the geography of faith was urban, and Christianity made a home in the lives of new believers across every strata of life. Rather than withdraw or become isolated from the city, the new believers were interwoven throughout urban life, and they thought about and wrestled with how to live their faith at work, in their communities, and in civic life.[6]

Their guiding principle in such matters, as the apostle Paul wrote in Colossians 3:17, was this: "Whatever you do, whether in word or deed, do it all in the name of the Lord Jesus, giving thanks to God the Father through him." All areas of urban life were to be conducted "in the name of Jesus";[7] that is, everything they encountered was to be turned toward Christ.[8] Faith wasn't just belief; it was an understanding of how all of life was to be lived under Christ. With gratitude to God as the Creator and Redeemer, the whole of life is given to the service of Christ.[9]

Learning to live their newly developing Christian faith at home, at work, and in their daily interactions was how the early church grew.

*   *   *

This pattern continues even today, with new questions and challenges. Whether bankers or teachers, social workers or taxi drivers, police officers or artists, entrepreneurs or retail workers, Christians are turning every area of their lives toward Christ. Whether they live and work in the bustling neighborhoods of Queens, where you can hear scores of different languages and dialects, smell an abundance of spices, and taste flavors in restaurants from the world over, or in Manhattan in the world of finance, amidst towering skyscrapers, Christians are making Christ's presence known. And in this, they are witnesses of the gospel alive in the city.

We can see this in the lives of Derrick and Alice, New Yorkers originally from Hong Kong, who attended Oversea Chinese Mission in Manhattan's Chinatown after college, in the early part of their professional careers. Over the past eight years, they have since lived in Tokyo, Shanghai, and Hong Kong. As they have moved from place to place, they have framed their work—strategic planning in the pharmaceutical industry and human resources in finance—as ministry. Wherever they go with their young son, they see their vocation and calling as helping others develop their gifts, and they see their home, work, and church life as integral to who they are and who they are becoming in these major Asian cities.

From one perspective, Biju, an ordained minister and trained engineer from India, used to work in housing and now works in public transportation here in New York City. But from another perspective, as Biju goes around the city, he interacts with people, praying as he goes, and does church work in his daily life.

Tony, who works on Wall Street in banking, seeks to bring his life and faith to bear on his relationships with family, colleagues, and friends, serving the city and metropolitan area over decades.

Gloria, who is originally from the Dominican Republic, works in Washington Heights as an ophthalmologist. As a mother, she raised her children and attended medical school. She went on to further study in theological education, and she has served in leadership in her church as well as in and through her medical practice.

*　　　*　　　*

Just as these New Yorkers have moved from place to place, following their vocation wherever they go, in Acts 8:4–8 we read how the church was scattered to new cities following the death of Stephen:

> Now those who were scattered went from place to place, proclaiming the word. Philip went down to the city of Samaria and proclaimed the Messiah to them. The crowds with one accord listened eagerly to what was said by Philip, hearing and seeing the signs that he did, for unclean spirits, crying with loud shrieks, came out of many who were possessed; and many others who were paralyzed or lame were cured. So there was great joy in that city.

The church grew through its movement into new cities and across cultural frontiers, and the result was the healing of lives. As people stay and live their faith in every area of life, including if not especially the world of work, there is joy in the city.

- In what ways do you see ministry and work overlap in your life? How have you inadvertently or intentionally separated the two?

- Think back on your past week, or even today. In what ways have you seen God provide opportunities for you to be a witness for the gospel—on the street, in the subway, at the office, or even at home? How is "ministry" blending in to every area of your life?

- What do you see as obstacles or challenges for you as you reflect on ways to bring together the notion of faith and work as integral in your life?

- Where have you seen joy in the city, in the lives of people living their faith out in the everyday?

Chapter 3

Art and Public Faith

As we were planning for a community arts installation at the Walls-Ortiz Gallery and Center, eight-year-old Precious had an idea. "What if we include a flower?" That flower became "How Does Our Garden Grow?"—an installation in our storefront gallery that grew over seven weeks into a garden of trees, covered with roots, flowers, leaves, and fruit, expressing the dreams, hopes, and expectations of our community; a bridge of shared inspiration, including a community-DJed playlist, a "family" scrapbook, and a portrait gallery of images and quotations; and a greenhouse-idea incubator, building on an earlier community collaboration, the Harlem Story Mapping Project. Precious and her mother, Faith, were part of a planning group—including seminary staff Anthony and Maria, longtime Harlem residents chaplain Adrienne and Sister Marylin, and April, a doctoral student from a nearby university researching arts-based conflict resolution—that designed and implemented this inaugural annual experiment in hospitality and public faith.

The city street is where life happens, as Jane Jacobs famously observed.[1] So we cross the thresholds of our doors and welcome that life inside. The gallery—named after Andrew Walls and Manuel Ortiz, exemplars of Christian ministry in our seminary community—has become integral to City Seminary's approach to arts-based theological education and to being a good neighbor as an institution. Our mission is to create a "third space" for interaction and connection through the arts in a changing neighborhood, a place where seminary and public life intersects amidst the diversity of cultures and people in our community.

Seminary faculty, staff, students, and volunteers regularly rotate through public visiting hours at the gallery, which is open four afternoons a week and one Saturday each month. We practice hospitality in getting to know our neighbors personally and at street level, whether it is spending time with families with young children who come by two or three times a week after school for impromptu art making, newcomers to the area, or longtime residents discovering us for the first time. Whoever it is who comes through the door, we have found that something unique unfolds when the arts are allowed to help us see ourselves and hear others. This is what it means to do theology on the street level, and for us to be a seminary in the city.

As the theologian N. T. Wright notes, Ephesians 2:10 says "we are *poema*, God's artwork, created in the Messiah for the good works which God wants us to do . . . these are the impact we have as individual poems, works of art."[2] Whether in the gallery or beyond, the art we are and the art we make form a testimony to God's work of a new creation in the world, in our community, and in the present.

*   *   *

Whether you are an artist or not, art is a part of everyday life in the city. Art and culture are part of what makes a city dynamic and alive. Cities are where great museums are located, concert halls and opera houses are established, theater and dance companies operate, public artwork is painted on walls and on monuments, and singers and musicians take to street corners and subway stops. And the architecture and planning of cities—its blocks, buildings, and greenspaces—engage us as whole persons.

But art and culture in the city are not just about works of art to be seen or heard. They can teach us about ways to see ourselves and hear others.

Joshua is a new media artist and teaches computer science at a private university in Manhattan, while his wife Sachi is a writer and librarian. His art ranges from collaborative performance work that explores faith and suffering to a video sculpture that explores place, navigation technologies, and modes of physical and ontological knowing. Sachi writes and reads poetry at a local venue in Queens. Together they are involved in healing prayer ministry at their Episcopal church in Manhattan, and they host a fellowship group in Queens. They take turns caring for their toddler son as they live out their faith as parents, artists, and educators. Joshua and Sachi have also been involved in mission work in Japan, connecting to Sachi's family roots and living the transnational nature of city life.

Jenny is a theater professor, director, and writer/editor of educational materials who is dedicated to cross-cultural exchange and building community through the arts and education. She is particularly interested in the ways in which her gifts in theater and her faith intersect—directing dramatic readings on themes such as apartheid and reconciliation in South Africa and collaborating with a neuroscientist on performance art, mirror neurons, and empathy—and how that leads to intergenerational community conversations at our seminary's gallery in Harlem.

Sister West is an artist in the way she designs and makes clothes with West African fabrics from her home country Nigeria. Whether she is serving as a ministry worker in her Pentecostal church or creating art in the fashion of her cultural traditions, Sister West is embracing her gifts of design and faith in the practice of ministry in the city.

Originally from Korea, Christina, an up-and-coming singer, pianist, and musical director, is working on her doctorate in music therapy while integrating her love for and talent in pop and R&B music with ministry. A Korean

American worshiping in a West Indian Pentecostal church, she is engaged in cross-cultural ministry—whether she is performing on television or recording with acclaimed Korean artists. From the nightclub to the church, her music and her faith are heard in the private and public spheres.

*　　　　*　　　　*

As we shared in the beginning of this chapter, the Walls-Ortiz Gallery is where we are learning about our faith in the city.

Through the gallery, we have held juried group exhibitions of local artists, hosted traveling exhibitions from South Africa and elsewhere, established relationships with local institutions like schools, senior homes, and community centers, hosted pop-up artisan fairs to support local entrepreneurs, and begun a series of free monthly community conversations. At these conversations, we invite neighbors—new and old in a changing Harlem—to welcome each other and introduce ourselves, share a meal, appreciate and respond to art, and make art together. We create a "third space" for listening and voicing our experiences, and neighbors come off the street with their groceries and sometimes their dogs. Some return time and again, having found new friends and a place to call home. Thus, the gallery has become a place of public faith, gathering, interaction, listening, local access, and hospitality.

Whether it is an exhibition featuring photography taken by youth in their neighborhoods around the city, a multimedia consideration of work as a curse or calling, or an exhibition focused on lament, hope, and restoration through photography, installation, and painting that explores incarceration, modern-day slavery, and racial justice, the gallery has made time and space for art to inspire, encourage, and challenge us to engage. Questions are raised that require us to "theologize" on the ground, thinking through how to respond to historical and contemporary issues with our faith in the forefront, conversations that begin in the gallery and spill out onto the street. This is the dynamic process of theological learning and thinking.

An installation facilitated by Myra, an artist in the neighborhood, was the Harlem Story Mapping Project, a space for stories to be heard and exchanged and for community collaboration to take place. It became the hub for memories and new experiences and an ongoing testament to the changes in the neighborhood, inviting all voices to be heard. It also became the starting point for the community arts installation series, described earlier.

As we welcome newcomers and regulars to the gallery, we have found that it has become a safe and "brave" space for difficult conversations and an acknowledged venue for mutuality in our neighborhood. Through the arts—whether we are hosting a musical performance or a dramatic reading, inviting school groups in for a hands-on arts collage or photography workshop, or facilitating an artist panel where diversity is the norm—we are practicing our faith and engaging in culture as an institutional good neighbor in our community.

Tradition has it that Luke, whom we consider an evangelist with an urban heart, was a painter, which is why he is the patron saint for artists. In this spirit, whether they are writing a play, being dedicated to the craft of an instrument, or expressing praise in worship and dance, Christians are using the arts to help build up and seek the peace of the city.

Just as a garden needs nourishment to grow, the Spirit has worked in ever-new ways, shapes, and forms to enable us to look at ourselves with reframed perspectives and to hear others with greater clarity. Through the arts, we are offering and experiencing mutual welcome, being transformed in the midst.

QUESTIONS TO CONSIDER

- How regularly do you notice the presence or impact of art—music, dance, drama, performance art, or visual art—in your daily life? What is its impact on you? Are you inspired, encouraged, or challenged to see things in a new light? Do you seek out such experiences?

- How often do you invite or welcome art to be a part of your life in the city? How easy or difficult is it to access art and culture? What obstacles prevent you from exploring these resources more often?

- Where are the spaces and places in your city that you find art and public faith intersect? Are there ways to create or cultivate opportunities for this?

Chapter 4

Make Yourselves at Home

I (Maria) was born in Ipswich, England, and came to the United States as a child. My parents, who had originally emigrated from Hong Kong to the United Kingdom, were part of a flow of Christian believers from the East and the South to the West, a reverse mission trajectory. In fact, they were the fruit of a significant college campus movement and revival in Hong Kong in the 1950s and 1960s, in part because of missionaries who had to leave China after 1950. They were immigrants living their faith wherever they were around the world.

Our family came to New York in the early 1980s, bringing with us a broadcasting ministry that served the immigrant Chinese community—not only in New York City (particularly the garment factory and restaurant workers who at the time could not attend church on Sundays) but also in the pockets of Chinese immigrants scattered all over the world—with a range of evangelistic programs recorded on cassette tapes in some ten or more different Chinese dialects. In New York, my parents joined a community of Chinese Christians living, working, and worshiping together in the city and surrounding suburbs, reaching across the subdivisions of an immigrant community, university-educated professionals along with blue-collar workers.

The church they attended in Manhattan's Chinatown, Oversea Chinese Mission, became one of the largest Chinese churches in the city, holding services in Mandarin, Cantonese, and English. It continues to minister to all sectors of the community, from English as a Second Language and citizenship classes to the praying elderly Sisters Fellowship and young families' ministries. New ministries, such as a Saturday basketball ministry for local youth, are thriving as subsequent generations take the helm of leadership. It is another example of these threads coming together to form the fabric of faith in New York City.

*   *   *

Jeremiah 29:4–7 is often read as a text about peacemaking, exile, and the city:

> This is what the LORD Almighty, the God of Israel, says to all those I carried into exile from Jerusalem to Babylon: "Build houses and settle down; plant gardens and eat what they produce. Marry and have sons and daughters; find wives for your sons and

give your daughters in marriage, so that they too may have sons and daughters. Increase in number there; do not decrease. Also, seek the peace and prosperity of the city to which I have carried you into exile. Pray to the LORD for it, because if it prospers, you too will prosper." (NIV)

As we see, this text is also about families. This applies to singles who are part of extended families as much as other family constellations. Seek the peace and flourishing of the city; settle and raise your family there.

One of things that makes raising a family in the city not just possible but a gift is the extended networks of family and friends. While I no longer attend the church I grew up in, making peace with my own calling to be a bridge-builder and to work cross-culturally, I have not left. My family and I remain deeply involved and attached to our spiritual family and ethnic community. My husband, Tony, who came to church through an afterschool program at True Light Lutheran Church in Chinatown, also attended Oversea Chinese Mission in high school and through the years before our marriage.

By retaining these ties, I am connected with friends, uncles and aunties, grandmothers and grandfathers, and even former students in this Chinese church world—a network of immigrant churches where people know one another, often removed by only two degrees of separation.

We say, "If you are Christian and Asian in New York City, you must know someone who knows someone."

Trust, camaraderie, and relationships mean that I, and others like me, have been able to reenter into this community with its multiple generations as insiders rather than outsiders. This opens up new relationships and ministry possibilities for families in the city. It enables me to walk together with new and old leaders in the church, as well as to make space at the seminary for conversations across immigrant communities, both newer and older. It means friendships that endure with my peers, like Mi and Eric, with whom I attended church as I grew up.

The seminary has hosted a series of gatherings for pastors, church workers, and leaders to come together to talk about the challenges and contributions of the immigrant Asian church. During these conversations, the tensions and complexities of multiple generations, cultures, and identities were raised. Family—in its unity and diversity—can be a wonderful and frustrating thing. Yet seeing the mix of intergenerational worship through the lens of stories rather than focusing on templates or role models for churches allows for flexibility to understand and explore best principles and values from a variety of contexts.[1] Listening to each other and making connections across diverse communities is something to treasure as an opportunity for growth and blessing.

For those who do not have extended family close by,

friends and church members in the city become a critical element of community. Parents' groups around the city, connected by church community and a common season of early child-rearing years, help families navigate how to live in and raise their children in the city. Whether it is the millennial generation congregation of Vision Church, an Asian American congregation on the Upper West Side, a daughter church of Oversea Chinese Mission, or others around the five boroughs that bring together perspectives from multiple generations on raising families, the time and space to explore questions, challenges, and resources make the commitment to stay in the city possible. Family goes beyond blood ties.

This also points to other ways that generations are at work in the immigrant church communities. These church communities serve as places of leadership development for young people—such as those in St. Luke's, a predominantly West Indian Episcopalian church in the Bronx, or Indian Pentecostal Church in Queens. They provide comfort in the familiar for the elderly, particularly in cultural communities found in Jackson Heights or Flushing, Queens. They provide critical social and spiritual resources for the newly arrived—for the newer wave of Chinese from Fuzhou at Grace Church in lower Manhattan, or the satellite "Little Fuzhou" in Brooklyn's Chinatown. In all of these contexts, they are hubs for generations to come home. It is a great gift to be able to learn across generations, ages, and experiences.

Following Jeremiah's words, perhaps instead of thinking about how we can raise a family in the city, or grow a church in the city, we should consider the ways in which working for a healthy and flourishing city enables us to raise a family and grow a church. In paying attention to what is in front of and around us—seeing our context, knowing our neighbors, listening to the concerns and the dreams of others—there are new possibilities to join in the cultivation of thriving communities that bear witness to what can and will be.

*   *   *

The typical city dweller spends time at home, at work, and at leisure in the city, but there is not always time to get to know the city in all its nuances. Going one block to the east or west can make a big difference in the demographics of the city. Yet how much do we know of others who are not like us, spending time intentionally building relationships that go beyond transaction and function? How much do we even know the streets and the people we pass by every day, walking to the subway, buying our morning coffee, or sitting on the bus? How can we love a city without knowing it?[2]

Miriam, whom we mentioned earlier, is doing just that with her family in Harlem and her church in the Bronx. As she leads the children's Sunday school out into the streets to pray and break bread with their neighbors, she works for the flourishing of her community.

Hiroko has been faithful for years in leading worship services with volunteers from different churches at a nearby nursing home. At the same time, she lives out her faith at work in information technology in the corporate sector, at home in Harlem, and in the city, involved also in supporting an arts non-profit organization.

Jimmy and Christine live in northern Manhattan. He leads a ministry restoring women who were victims of human trafficking, and she serves as a priest in an Episcopal church known to serve and welcome executives, artists, and the homeless. Hosting "Fred" talks—that is, "Ted talks with friends"—on hot topics on Friday evenings, they welcome young professionals in their twenties and thirties for dinner and conversation in a safe and entertaining space, crossing generations in a different way.

Adebisi and Abosede are pastors with the Redeemed Christian Church of God in Bedford-Stuyvesant. Adebisi also works on Wall Street with a major insurance firm and runs a non-profit organization for youth leadership development, and Abosede is a businesswoman. While all of their children are now adults and have gone on to pursue their own careers, this couple has hosted young people from Nigeria for years, providing a home within their home as they help them transition to a new country and culture, welcoming them into their family. Interacting with the local and the global dynamics of the city, Adebisi and Abosede are staying to make a home for those without.

* * *

Returning to my own story, on a recent Father's Day I returned to the same bleachers I had sat on some twenty years earlier, while Tony (my friend then, and husband now) played in a basketball tournament. On this Father's Day, in the basement gym of a local public school, multiple generations who were part of Overseas Chinese Mission challenged each other on the court. Our former youth group counselor cheered on his son, who was playing against players twice his age, while my children half his age rooted for their dad on the sidelines. It hit me: no matter where or with whom I worshiped, this was home.

Staying in the city includes families. In ways that may be surprising, the city can support the flourishing of families. And as we stay in the city as families, supporting its thriving, we bring God glory and honor in ways that challenge old stereotypes about city life and establish new ways for the church to grow.

QUESTIONS TO CONSIDER

- What makes the city a good place to raise a family? How can it also be challenging to do this well?

- Whom do you know, or whom have you come across in books or other places, that is an example of perseverance for the greater good? What aspects of their work are an encouragement to you? Where do you see obstacles for yourself?

- If you were to draw a map of your own life, where God has placed you before the present and where you are being led, what would it look like? Do you imagine staying rather than going as a possible future?

Chapter 5

The Next Generation

Summer is a special time of the year for Indian Diaspora Pentecostal Christians living in the New York metro area. Geomon, the pastor of one such Indian diaspora church, knows firsthand. On the weekends, young and old alike gather at different churches and school auditoriums for a time of revival meetings, church conventions, and seminars. It is an opportunity for people to connect and reconnect after the long winter. For these meetings, women exchange American clothing for Indian attire of a *saree* or a *salwar*. This festive season is a time of prayer, worship, and celebration of God's work in families, churches, and communities.

During one such summer meeting ten years ago, a group of young people from the First Church of God, an Indian Pentecostal church with one foot in the borough of Queens and the other in the broader metropolitan region, helped to birth a new vision for ministry. As they entered adulthood, they were beginning to take responsibility for the faith of their generation.

They first launched a ministry called Re-mix, bridging old and new ways of worship and community life for their peers. A few years later, the group began the Community Worship Service, a church within the church intended for the second generation and the surrounding community. The young people of the First Church of God had experienced a living and joyful faith, and they were committed to both honoring their history and adapting its ways to a new time.

*   *   *

From parents to pastors to denominational leaders, there is great concern about what will happen to young people. Will they stay in the church or leave? Will they retain their faith or set it aside? Will they experience joy in the midst of growing up in the city?[1] Such questions are contemporary and ancient (Deut. 6:4–9), for the transmission of faith from one generation to the next is the only way the church will continue.[2] There is no single way this is happening, but we see many hopeful signs of ways in which the gospel is being passed on, is being received, and is growing. Overall, we see churches seeking to instill in their youth a sense of seriousness to Christian purpose, life, and vocation. Churches are not only working to retain their young people but also encouraging them to follow Christ in mission, calling, and purpose.

A wonderful example is in the South Bronx among Catholic parishes, where we see a great commitment by parents and leaders. During a recent year at one parish, cared for by priests from Argentina and sisters from Mexico, over four hundred children and young people were part of the confirmation class. The parish is understaffed, so there is of course more work to be done in areas of youth leadership and formation, but this does not take away from how families view their parish and want to support their children in a faith journey.

In Manhattan, a new generation of young people with family histories in Africa is doing something remarkable. Meeting in rented space at a performing artists center in Manhattan, Desire of Nations Church is filled with young adults, encompassing all professions and educational backgrounds in New York. It was launched a few years ago as a spinoff from the International Center, a Redeemed parish in Brooklyn. Rather than just keep expanding, which the International Center is still doing, the Brooklyn parish created space for the young professionals who grew up in the church to begin a new church of their own. Desire of Nations emphasizes not only individual growth in life and faith but also reaching others in the city. There is an intention for diversity of cultures built into their work from the start.

Paul wrote to the church in Colossae, "So then, just as you received Christ Jesus as Lord, continue to live in him, rooted and built up in him, strengthened in the faith as you were taught, and overflowing with thankfulness" (Col. 2:6–7 NIV; see also Eph. 3:16–19). Being rooted in Christ enables growth while being nourished in freedom and gratitude.

"Rooted and built up" is a key image we have seen at Redeemed and elsewhere. Holding on to the key commitments they learned in their home church, young people most often flourish in churches where young leaders have the freedom to try new things. This acknowledges the role of faith and culture in their home church, but also gives room to grow in new cultural settings. Finding the right balance requires pastoral wisdom and a commitment to listening.[3]

*　　　*　　　*

In the mid-1940s in Chicago, second-generation immigrants from Sweden and Norway saw a need to serve their next generation. Aiming to address needs at the national level as well as the local, one of the groups they founded was Youth for Christ, and one of its first employees was an evangelist named Billy Graham.[4]

Could something similar be happening on a national level today? Quite possibly. This time it will not be Swedes, but Indians, Nigerians, Latinos, Koreans, and others from around the world. Whole new movements may emerge to shape generations to come, across ethnic and cultural lines.

New Christian youth movements are one example. Indian Pentecostal churches, especially those with links to Kerala, have founded the Pentecostal Youth Fellowship of America, which began in New York City and spread to other cities, such as Dallas, as Indian church families moved across the country. The Pentecostal Conference of North American Keralites has its own youth forum. The Redeemed Christian Church of God has a national program called Youth Aflame, and the Damascus Christian Church also has national and international youth councils.

As diverse as these new Christian youth movements are, they all place great emphasis on worship, reading the Bible, prayer, community, sharing how God turns up in their lives, and developing future life goals. They find strength in being part of an intergenerational community, listening to and learning from one another with mutuality and respect in Christ. Practices that have been learned to sustain Christian faith are passed on, generation by generation.

We are thankful to God for the leaders who have sacrificed so much for so many years to found churches across our city and the urban world. They have provided a home for young people to experience the gospel. As they now listen to the next generation, they trust that the same God who led them will lead their children and grandchildren and help them discover and live their gifts. For the next generation are the future inhabitants of our growing cities. They stay in the city, raising their families, praying and working for the flourishing of their city—for it is their home.

QUESTIONS TO CONSIDER

- Can you think of other examples of young people you have met, or come across, to add to these exciting and hopeful stories of the church alive?

- What are ways that you can encourage those around you, young people in particular, to see their potential lived out in faith? How can young people be encouraged and supported to discover and express their gifts?

- How can the generations support one another in your church?

Chapter 6

Lessons for the Long Run

O ne of our favorite places to go with our families in the city is a small island eight hundred feet off the southern tip of Manhattan. Over the years, this island has had many names and uses. The Lenape tribe knew it as Pagganuck; later, Dutch settlers called it Nutten Island, after its nut trees. In the eighteenth century, the British made it a military base and called it Governor's Island. In later years, it became a United States Coast Guard base. And when the Coast Guard base was eventually closed, the then-abandoned island was filled with vacant buildings, empty housing, and even a shuttered Burger King.[1]

In 2003, the federal government sold the island to New York City for a dollar, but it stipulated that its use had to be for the public good. A trust was formed for redevelopment, a Dutch landscape architect was hired to chart a new vision, and public and private resources were pooled to improve the island.

Today, Governor's Island is a place for play, recreation,

and budding economic life. After a short ferry ride, adults and children play on slides down a big hill, ride bikes or rest on a hammock, attend an arts festival, buy a cold drink or relish a serving of jerk chicken from street vendors.[2] The island's views of the Manhattan skyline, Brooklyn, Staten Island, and the Statue of Liberty, the symbol of America's welcome to immigrants from around the world, are breathtaking. Play, inspiration, rest, and movement are all there and are ways the city can nourish its inhabitants. But of course it took hard work, planning, and a vision that is still ongoing and unfolding.

*   *   *

For the past several years, as part of our work to understand the practices of ministry in the city, we have been gathering what we have been learning about sustainable and fruitful ministry in the city from New York City, North America, and all over the world. During this time, we held a series of conversations with over forty ministry leaders, pastors, educators, and Christians in diverse professions and life settings around the theme of ministry in the city. Having reviewed the data across all of our conversations, we have heard in our conversations a template of important themes and practices for how good, sustainable, and flourishing ministry in the city occurs. There is no single pathway of ministry in an ever-changing city, but there are approaches and processes that make a difference.

Lesson 1—Begin with What Is in Front of You

As the story of Governor's Island shows us, ministry in the city begins with what is right in front of us, perhaps right under our feet or just out of the way, and it unfolds in ways that fit into the context. Look around, pray, think, share this journey with others, wait on the Spirit, try to see afresh what is right in front of you, and take the time that is needed. Because no two settings, neighborhoods, or cities are alike, the gospel takes shape in the local context. Whatever city or neighborhood you are in, beauty and ministry, the energies of the Spirit and the city, go together. When the work that is done fits the context, it will come from within, not from without.

Lesson 2—Relationships Come First

Starting a new church, creating affordable housing, feeding the poor, training youth pastors, advocating for a cause, addressing legal issues that face refugees and immigrants—these are some of the very concrete needs that ministry seeks to address. But if there is one theme we have heard over and over, it is that the heart of ministry is not solving a large societal problem or launching a new church, however significant those are, but being attentive to and valuing relationships. This is especially true when we see cities as complexly interconnected relationships, cultures, networks, and institutions. The theologian and educator Ruth Padilla-DeBorst emphasizes relationships of listening, learning, and giving testimony to the impact of people and their presence in community.

Relationships place a priority and a premium on time, people, building community, and patience. Programs, staff, and planning can have an important place in ministry in the city, but relationships are the foundation and the key to longevity and sustainability. This is true in work of all professions, community development in the neighborhood, and pastoral leadership at all levels. And this reminds us that, most of all, cities are about people and stories.

In every type of church, young people tell us that what really matters are relationships. Irene Cho, who works with youth groups in Los Angeles and other cities, has made this central to the work she does. Whether speaking at conferences, writing curricula, or researching the experiences of urban and suburban youth from demographically homogenous and diverse communities, she has found that family, youth workers, and young people themselves are all integral to "sticky faith."[3]

Getting things done and even changed, especially

amidst institutons, requires networking and building long-term relationships. Luke Bretherton, who is originally from London and now lives in Durham where he teaches at Duke Divinity School, knows this to be true as a result of the community organizing work he has participated in and observed.

In a neighborhood in north Philadelphia, Debbie Ortiz-Vasquez is a lawyer and community advocate working within the setting of a faith-based community health center. She is imagining and engaging in new ways with her colleagues what it means to practice holistic care for patients' and their families' health and well-being—social, mental, spiritual, and otherwise. And it begins with relationships that are personal and individual as well as community-wide.

Of course, even as we prioritize relationships and recognize the interruptions that come with divine potential every day, we also have to find ways to manage the priorities and responsibilities each of us hold. That is one of the reasons we need a community to help us discern.

Lesson 3—Community Matters

Ministry in the city is not just what we do as individuals but what is accomplished as part of communities. In the context of the city, our local pockets of community support us and remind us of what is important. Our community can be our family, a small group, or our worshiping congregation. For pastors and church workers, community can be a support system of peers that helps sustain us in healthy and thriving ministry.

Community is the context for forgiveness, for vulnerability, and for unpacking our experiences. As the Uganadan priest and Notre Dame professor Emmanuel Katongole stresses, community is also a place for lament. It is for sharing suffering and hardship, for not carrying our burdens alone. As such, community is integral to establishing resilience in ministry.[4]

In a raw week of early July 2016, as the world saw videos of African American men shot and killed by police in Baton Rouge and Minnesota and then learned of police being killed by a sniper in Dallas, chaplain and pastor Adrienne Croskey, the director of Fresh Oils Ministries in Harlem, opened the doors for a time of sharing what people were feeling, followed by prayer. It was a space for community.

Urban life can be intense and tiring, often exhausting. Many know Jude Tiersma-Watson as a wise faculty member at Fuller Theological Seminary, but at least as much a part of her life are the church and mission communities she belongs to in Los Angeles. Being aware of the pace and intensity of urban life, Jude has also emphasized observing the Sabbath, spending time with God through devotions or prayer, and reserving time for family, leisure, and work.

She has authored online and print resources to support the work of urban youth workers who are interacting with the "environmental press" of the city.[5]

Community is where we pray, hear one another, wrestle with Scripture, and go forward in ministry together. It is where we can be, and become, more human.

Lesson 4—Try New Things, Take Risks

Ministry in the city is about trying new things, taking risks, making mistakes, finding new ways of doing things through continual learning. For if the practice of ministry begins with waiting on God, it is also about being ready when the Spirit moves and the time is right for acting. The work of innovation, creativity, and risk taking most commonly starts with small steps that grow into bigger and unexpected ones. We may be looking one way, but God is looking backward, forward, and to the present into our lives and experiences.

In 2009, the high school youth group led by Daniel Sanabria of Christian Tabernacle, a Latino Pentecostal church in Park Slope, Brooklyn, organized a prayer walk across Manhattan. Called God Belongs in My City, the walk continues every October, and more than one thousand young people from some two hundred Pentecostal churches in the city walk (or longboard) across the streets of Manhattan from Harlem and the Battery to Times Square, praying, singing, blowing trumpets, laughing, texting, tweeting, and posting photos on Instagram and Facebook as they go. It is a day of joyful life that ends with kneeling in prayer on the streets of the city for the flourishing of the city—their city. And what began in Brooklyn has now inspired similar youth movements in eighty cities nationally and globally.

In the city of Baltimore, Van Gardner had just retired after a long and successful tenure leading the Cathedral of the Incarnation Episcopal Church. But instead of just watching the Orioles play baseball, Van and his wife Kathy took on the nearly cathedral-sized St. Luke's Episcopal Church in West Baltimore, which was about to be shuttered. The immensity of the challenge to establish a new ministry and save the building in a neighborhood at such great risk is profound, but working with a remaining core of members and having cultivated a life in God and ministry in the city, Van and Kathy embraced it. And friends like John and Ana Kiess, who live and work in Baltimore, have joined in this work. Keeping it all going is day to day, relying only on volunteers. Yet for John, who teaches theology at Loyola University, St. Luke's is a place of energy and life like none other.

Billy Vo lives in Seattle and is involved in equipping Asian American leaders in the church. He is also committed to his city, to creating a "third space" for outreach in a socio-economically diverse neighborhood—an exercise gym with an income-scaled access fee plan where relationships can lead to unexpected futures in the life of the gospel.

As these stories from New York, Baltimore, and Seattle show us, being open to the future means first of all being aware of our local context and environment. Out of this, we are invited to be creative, innovative, and entrepreneurial. This is also a good pathway to the resources we need: resources follow vision, which at its best builds on the relationships and work that have been established and are starting to grow.

Of course, while trying something new and risky can be exciting, we are always going to make mistakes and are ever faced with the possibility of what seems like failure. But experience and experts show us that reflecting on and learning from failure are the processes by which new knowledge and practice are developed. And in the reign of God, we can't always see how God is connecting the pieces of stories. Our lives, churches, and ministries belong to God.

Lesson 5—Who You Are Is Significant

The final lesson we have heard is that it's not just the plans or designs for ministry that we come up with that matter: who you are as leaders is what matters most. Self-awareness, the interior life of the believer, recognition that we can't do anything without God, gratitude, humility, patience, commitment, the willingness to forgive, transparency, and other areas of personal character are critical to living fully into one's vocation and calling.

As the director of the Urban Youth Workers Institute, Larry Acosta has a passion for youth ministry. But what he stresses is the life of the person in leadership and ministry. Are leaders accountable to others? Do they turn to others for help?

Kathy Maskell is pastor of discipleship at Blue Route Vineyard Church. Moving from New York to a small town in Pennsylvania, Kathy knows a diversity of settings. In her pastoral work, she emphasizes the importance of growing in the Spirit, of hearing the voice of the Spirit.

Who we are in Christ, and how we are attending to our journey, matters profoundly to ministry in the city.

*   *   *

The practice of ministry in the city is never abstract, but flows out of a realization of God's love for us and our world in Christ. Worship, Scripture, and prayer are paramount. So where we end is also the foundation to begin.

QUESTIONS TO CONSIDER

- What do you think are the opportunities and obstacles for you, as you think about living, staying, and ministering in the city?

- What questions does this raise for you, as you reflect on your own context in the city? What opportunities are there around you to live into a particular lesson that might resonate with you?

- Who are the people around you, or those you hope to get to know better, that could walk with you prayerfully into possibilities that God has for working together, in mutuality?

Epilogue: Joy in the City

C hrist has risen. The Spirit has come. The city is changing, the street ever dynamic, full of aspirations and
urgent concerns. Love this city! Find God's joy! Stay in the
city! See what God will do!

These are the voices we hear from the witness of Manny
Ortiz and Sue Baker, who were partners in the work of the
gospel for over forty years. In 1987, after church-planting
and ministry development in Chicago with their respec-
tive families, Manny and Blanca Ortiz and Sue and Randy
Baker experienced God's call to Philadelphia.

With their families, Manny and Sue began Spirit and
Truth Fellowship in north Philadelphia, and over the years
they developed leaders and nine neighborhood churches.
Across the street from a traditional church building that
had become the sanctuary of Spirit and Truth and also
served as a Christian school, they renovated an old warehouse and called it Joy in the City. At Joy in the City, they
built classrooms and trained leaders for the church and

neighborhoods of Philadelphia. On the street side of their building, Simple Cycle opened, a bike shop for the neighborhood. Next door, a new center of the dynamic Esperanza Health Center was opened in their neighborhood, on land formerly owned by Spirit and Truth.

Manny and Sue stayed in the city, keeping their commitments and relationships. They shared their resources with others and persisted in the city in spite of many challenges. Out of their love for Christ's church in the city, they emphasized the importance of an incarnational and prayerful life. Grounded in Scripture, they concentrated on their neighborhood and its experiences. They worked for God's peace and reconciliation amidst the divisions in their city. They committed themselves to the next generation of leaders. They shared the life-changing power of Jesus with everyone they met in the city. They trusted in a sovereign God.

As we were completing this book, Manny's life came to a close. From across the city and around the country, people came to give thanks to God for his life, for the way he had stayed in the city with prayerful purpose each hour, day, and week. In spite of the large numbers expected to attend, instead of having the memorial service somewhere away from the church in a space large enough to hold everyone, it was held in the neighborhood, in the sanctuary of Spirit and Truth. The overflow space was across the street in the gym and conference rooms at Esperanza. Manny knew where God had called him, and so did his community and family. He was a neighborhood pastor.

When we stay in the city, we don't know what God will do, what we will see afresh or encounter. But God has invited all of us to stay in the city, to wait to receive power from on high, the gift of the Spirit, and to trust how God is already at work. The Spirit works in the city through the church, from the blocks we walk to the bike lanes we travel; from the businesses where we work, to the markets we shop in, to the art we have conversations around; from the families we are a part of, to the young people who inspire us, and to the daily contact we make with others familiar and strange in our midst. God works through the everyday and is with us in the everyday. Staying and waiting on the Spirit cultivates patience, humility, a sense of grace, and time for the journey we share.

Returning to those we described in our opening chapter, Vivian and Beverly, Kari Jo and Cory, Peter and Miriam, Sister Marylin, Melissa and Andy, and Rex, as well as the many others we have borne witness to here—all of them have helped us to see that the city is a vital and vibrant context for faith, life, and the practice of ministry. It is simply home for them and for untold millions more. God is calling them to stay in the city, with conviction that the possibilities for the kingdom are here, in the present and future. Their lives are witnesses to urban Christianity in the twenty-first century. They are living their faith every day in the city.

In our waiting in the city, our prayer is that our everyday God be with us. Renewed and refreshed in the love of Christ and the joy of the Spirit, we stay in the city for the purpose of the blessing and healing of our world. We join those who cry for peace, who in the Spirit are filled with expectation for the present and future of our urban world, God's creation.

In John 7:38, Jesus says, "Out of the believer's heart shall flow rivers of living water." This living water, as the theologian Rowan Williams reminds us, is the joy of the Spirit, "the sense that we are connected with something so real that it will break every boundary or container we try to confine it in, a sense of something overflowing, pushing outwards."[1] As we stay in the city, as God's people and works of art, let our joy spill into the street, ever moving in and through our communities, for God's peace.

Praise be to Jesus, who, from the starfields to the cities, is Lord of all.

QUESTIONS TO CONSIDER

- In what ways do you see God's invitation to you to stay and be present to the opportunities for gospel work in your home, in your work context, or in your neighborhood?

- How have you seen God at work in your life and context already? What difference might considering attentiveness, time, presence, prayer, and humility make in your own story?

- Who are the witnesses to the gospel in your city that help you understand God's call? How have they impacted you?

- What questions do you have now that you did not consider before?

Afterword

As pastors and lifelong New Yorkers, we want to commend *Stay in the City* for its vision of what ministry in the city looks like in the twenty-first century. Mark and Maria have given us a fresh look at how the Spirit is leading God's church in living out its calling in our urban world.

Stay in the City also gives us a glimpse into the lives of some of the people and churches City Seminary of New York has come alongside, creating community and enhancing our ministry experience.

This is a book that can open our understanding and clarify our misunderstandings of God's church in the urban context. Here we also find new and creative ways to engage our communities and learn about what God is doing in our city.

Stay in the City has encouraged us, and we pray it will encourage you, in the midst of what may seem like chaos, to shine where you are. Our prayer is that *Stay in the City* will inspire urban Christians, pastors, youth workers, and leaders to step back and reflect on how all of us can make and are making a difference in the city for Christ through the Spirit that gives new life.

PETER AND MIRIAM YVETTE ACEVEDO

Acknowledgments

We begin with thanks to God for this opportunity to share our story of how we have come to see and celebrate God's work in the midst of the city.

Stay in the City was composed out of the life and experience of City Seminary of New York. It truly belongs to our entire community, from our faculty and staff, to our board members, our students, our advocates and partners, and our Harlem neighbors, to all who have walked with us in prayer and friendship. A special thanks to Sachi Clayton, who read this more than once. We are grateful in particular to Miriam Acevedo, Geomon George, and our staff at the seminary for your friendship and support to help us finish the book.

We are grateful for the Practices working group members who shared their stories with us.

This book would not have been possible without the support and encouragement of John Wimmer, Chris Coble, and the Lilly Endowment, who have generously supported our work. We are grateful for their vision of a flourishing church in the city.

Thank you, David Bratt and everyone at Eerdmans, for this opportunity and for your commitment to excellence in Christian publishing and scholarship.

Bethia Liu enabled us to visualize the connections between our ideas, and Stephen Fowl helped us see key biblical connections.

Rita, Peter, and Daniel—you are part of this story in every way.

Tony, Joshua, Josiah, and Immy—we could not have done this without you.

The imprint of our friends Dr. Sue Baker and the late Manny Ortiz are across this book. It is our privilege to dedicate this book to Sue, who has stayed in the city.

More about City Seminary of New York

The mission of City Seminary of New York is to seek God's peace in our neighborhood, city, and world through theological education. An intercultural and inter-generational institution of theological learning focused on the practice of ministry, we learn through prayer, hospitality, the study of Scripture, the arts, and applied research. In programming that runs throughout the week and year, we look and listen to see what God is doing in the city, the gifts, visions, and communities where Christ is being formed. Learning from and with each other—at home, at work, at school, and on the streets—we experience a transformation by the Spirit. Through this process, we nurture the life and practice of Christian faith in the city for the next generation.

To learn more about City Seminary and our work on the practices of ministry in the city, visit our website at www.cityseminaryny.org. You can also contact us at mark@cityseminaryny.org.

Notes

Introduction

1. For a brief introduction to Luke and Acts, see Justo L. González, *The Story Luke Tells: Luke's Unique Witness to the Gospel* (Grand Rapids: Eerdmans, 2015).

2. The idea of Luke's "great commission" as both urban and "already being dispersed" is drawn from an unpublished sermon of Harvie M. Conn. For further background, see Harvie M. Conn, "Lucan Perspectives and the City," *Missiology* 13, no. 4 (1985): 409–28.

3. Note the study of C. Kavin Rowe, *World Upside Down: Reading Acts in the Graeco-Roman Age* (New York: Oxford University Press, 2009).

4. See David F. Ford's discussion of Luke and Acts in *Christian Wisdom: Desiring God and Learning in Love* (Cambridge: Cambridge University Press, 2007), 15–40.

5. This phrase and idea come from Julie Ault, *Come Alive! The Spirited Art of Sister Corita* (London: Four Corner Books, 2006). We thank Bethia Liu for drawing our attention to Sister Corita and her importance for our work.

6. Michael Kimmelman, "The Craving for Public Squares," *New York Review of Books*, April 7, 2016, 18. For statistical data, see a wide range of resources available online by the United Nations, including *World Urbanization Prospects: The 2014 Revision* (New York: United Nations, 2014).

7. Patrick Sisson, "New Report Shows Millennials Are Leaving Coastal Cities, Choosing Central Ones," *Curbed,* November 15, 2016, https://www.curbed.com/2016/11/15/13636814/rental-apartment -moving-millenial-report (accessed November 18, 2016).

8. Darryl T. Cohen, "Popular Trends in Incorporated Places: 2000–2013," *Current Population Reports,* United States Census Bureau, https://www.census.gov/content/dam/Census/library/publications /2015/demo/p25-1142.pdf (retrieved November 30, 2016).

9. On the range and types of cities, see Paul Knox, ed., *Atlas of Cities* (Princeton: Princeton University Press, 2014), and R. Burdett and D. Sudjic, *The Endless City* (New York: Phaidon, 2008).

10. Jennifer Robinson, *Ordinary Cities: Between Modernity and Development* (London: Routledge, 2006).

11. Saskia Sassen, "Cities: A Window into Larger and Smaller Worlds," *European Educational Research Journal* 11, no. 1 (2012): 1–10.

12. http://www.un.org/millenniumgoals/.

13. Saskia Sassen, "Cities Are at the Center of Our Environmental Future," *Sapiens* 2, no. 3 (2010): 2–8.

14. See Neil Brenner, "The 'Urban Age' in Question," *International Journal of Urban and Regional Research* 38, no. 3 (2014): 731–55.

15. Peter Kearns, "Learning Cities on the Move," *Australian Journal of Adult Learning* 55, no. 1 (April 2015): 153–68.

16. Wayne A. Meeks, *The First Urban Christians: The Social World of the Apostle Paul* (New Haven: Yale University Press, 1983), and Paul Trebilco, "Early Christian Communities in the Greco-Roman City: Perspectives on Urban Ministry from the New Testament," *Ex Auditu* 29 (2013): 25–48.

17. We recognize this terminology is limited, but we use it as shorthand to describe the range of Christian traditions.

18. Douglas A. Hall with Judy Hall and Steve Daman, *The Cat and the Toaster: Living System Ministry in a Technological Age* (Eugene, OR: Wipf and Stock, 2010).

19. See Maria Liu Wong, "Engaging the *Telos* and Sharing Tales of Theological Education," Theological Education Between the Times, Spotlight on Theological Education, *Religious Studies News*, April

2017, 19–22, and Christian Scharen and Sharon Miller, "Bright Spots in Theological Education: Hopeful Stories in a Time of Crisis and Change," *Auburn Studies* 22 (2016).

20. We are following on the work of Dorothy Bass and Craig Dykstra. See Dorothy C. Bass, ed., *Practicing Our Faith: A Way of Life for Searching People* (Grand Rapids: Eerdmans, 1997), Dorothy C. Bass and Craig Dykstra, eds., *For Life Abundant: Practical Theology, Theological Education, and Christian Ministry* (Grand Rapids: Eerdmans, 2008), and Craig Dykstra, "A Way to Live: Reflections on Dorothy Bass's Contributions to the Practice of Christian Faith and Life," *The Cresset* 77, no. 5 (2014): 26–27, 33–34.

21. For this framework across Scripture, see Bruce W. Winter, *Seek the Welfare of the City: Christians as Benefactors and Citizens* (Grand Rapids: Eerdmans, 1994).

22. Chris Argyris and Donald A. Schön, *Theory in Practice: Increasing Professional Effectiveness* (San Francisco: Jossey-Bass, 1974).

23. On the complexity and challenges of urban life, see Robert Kegan, *In Over Our Heads* (Cambridge, MA: Harvard University Press, 1998), and Ronald Heifetz, *Leadership without Easy Answers* (Cambridge, MA: Harvard University Press, 1994). On double-loop and triple-loop learning, see Argyris and Schön, *Theory in Practice*, and Joop Swieringa and Andre Wierdsma, *Becoming a Learning Organization: Beyond the Learning Curve* (Wokingham: Addison-Wesley, 1992).

24. For similar approaches, see the vital work of the Centro de Estudios Teológicos Interdisciplinarios (CETI) in Latin America and Dietrich Bonhoeffer, *Ethics*, translated from the German edition edited by Ilse Tödt, Heinz Eduard Tödt, Ernst Feil, and Clifford Green; English edition edited by Clifford Green, translated by Reinhard Krauss, Charles C. West, and Douglas W. Stott, Dietrich Bonhoeffer Works, 6 (Minneapolis: Fortress, 2005), 47–75.

Chapter 1

1. Abdoumaliq Simone, *City Life from Jakarta to Dakar* (New York: Routledge, 2010).

2. Wayne A. Meeks, *The First Urban Christians: The Social World of the Apostle Paul* (New Haven: Yale University Press, 1983).

3. Steve Fowl has greatly aided our framing in this reflection.

4. As a recent Pew study documents, the majority of immigrants to the United States are Christians. The study is available online at http://www.pewforum.org/2013/05/17/the-religious-affiliation-of-us-immigrants/.

5. On how first-century networks and extended communities played a significant role in the transmission of faith, see Meeks, *The First Urban Christians*, 74–110.

6. Mark R. Gornik, *Word Made Global: Stories of African Christianity in New York City* (Grand Rapids: Eerdmans, 2011).

7. David Gonzalez, "A Sliver of a Storefront, a Faith on the Rise," *The New York Times*, January 14, 2007, http://www.nytimes.com/2007/01/14/nyregion/14storefront.html?_r=0. See also Liz Robbins, "An Evangelical Revival in the Heart of New York," *The New York Times*, July 9, 2015. http://www.nytimes.com/2015/07/10/nyregion/central-park-festival-to-highlight-new-yorks-vibrant-evangelical-movement.html?_r=0.

8. Andrew F. Walls, *The Cross-Cultural Process in Christian History* (Maryknoll: Orbis Books, 2002).

Chapter 2

1. On vocation, see Tim Clydesdale, *The Purposeful Graduate: Why Colleges Must Talk to Students about Vocation* (Chicago: University of Chicago Press, 2015). See also Mark R. Schwehn and Dorothy C. Bass, eds., *Leading Lives That Matter: What We Should Do and Who We Should Be* (Grand Rapids: Eerdmans, 2006).

2. For a range of resources on faith and work, see the Theology of Work Project, www.theologyofwork.org.

3. See Sassen in "Redefining Notions of Urban Intelligence," *Live Mint*, September 20, 2016 E-Paper, http://www.livemint.com/Specials/m21w1rzMM8KpbE9KO1iFVK/Redefining-notions-of-urban-intelligence.html.

4. Abdoumaliq Simone, *City Life from Jakarta to Dakar: Movements at the Crossroads* (New York: Routledge, 2010).

5. Rowe, *World Upside Down*, 91–137.

6. See Richard Last, "The Neighborhood (*vicus*) of the Corinthian *ekklēsia*: Beyond Family-Based Descriptions of the First Urban Christ-Believers," *Journal for the Study of the New Testament* 38, no. 4 (2016): 399–425.

7. John M. G. Barclay, *Pauline Churches and Diaspora Jews* (Tübingen: Mohr Siebeck, 2011), 26–28.

8. This is Andrew Walls's notion of the relationship between culture and conversion.

9. On faith as understanding, see Barclay, *Pauline Churches*, 28. For life as service, see *Pauline Churches*, 254.

Chapter 3

1. Jane Jacobs, *The Life and Death of Great American Cities* (New York: Vintage Books, 1992).

2. N. T. Wright, "The Letter to the Ephesians," *Theology in Scotland* 20, no. 2 (2013): 9.

Chapter 4

1. Mitchell Kim and David Lee, "Intergenerational Ministry: Why Bother?," in *Honoring the Generations: Learning with Asian North American Congregations*, ed. M. Sydney Park, Soong-Chan Rah, and Al Tizon (Valley Forge, PA: Judson Press, 2012).

2. Robert Linthicum, "Learning How to Love Your City," *Together*, July–September 1991, 22.

Chapter 5

1. Thanks to Skip Masback for making this question vital for every church to ask, and for seeking to live it out in his ministry.

2. See Vern Bengtson with Norella M. Putney and Susan Harris, *Families and Faith: How Religion Is Passed Down across Generations* (New York: Oxford University Press, 2013), and Carolyn Chen and Russell Jueng, eds., *Sustaining Faith Traditions: Race, Ethnicity, and Religion among the Latino and Asian American Second Generation* (New York: NYU Press, 2012). For other background matters, see Nancy Foner, ed., *Across Generations: Immigrant Families in America* (New York: NYU Press, 2009).

3. Brother Jasper of Taizé, "Transmitting the Message of the Gospel to Youth," *International Review of Mission* 103, no. 2 (November 2014): 227–39.

4. We owe this example to Joel Carpenter, director of the Nagel Institute at Calvin College.

Chapter 6

1. This summary is drawn from Nick Paumgarten, "Useless Beauty," *The New Yorker*, August 31, 2009, 56–65.

2. See https://govisland.com/, and Alexandra Lange, "Play Ground," *The New Yorker*, May 16, 2016, 68–76.

3. http://stickyfaith.org/.

4. Christine D. Pohl, *Living into Community: Cultivating Practices That Sustain Us* (Grand Rapids: Eerdmans, 2012).

5. http://fulleryouthinstitute.org/urban/toolkit.

Epilogue

1. Rowan Williams, *Being Disciples: Essentials of the Christian Life* (Grand Rapids: Eerdmans, 2016), 85.